I0414292

Butterflies, beetles, and Bugs: A Coloring book

The materials in this book may be reproduced for personal use only. No part of this publication may be transmitted, stored, or recorded in any form without written permission from the author. For more information regarding permissions and other books by this author, visit www.kndbooks.com.

© 2017 Kerrian Neu. All rights reserved.

Design and illustration by Kerrian Neu.

ISBN   1548331120
ISBN-13   978-1548331122

kerrian neu design
print/web design & illustration

www.kndbooks.com

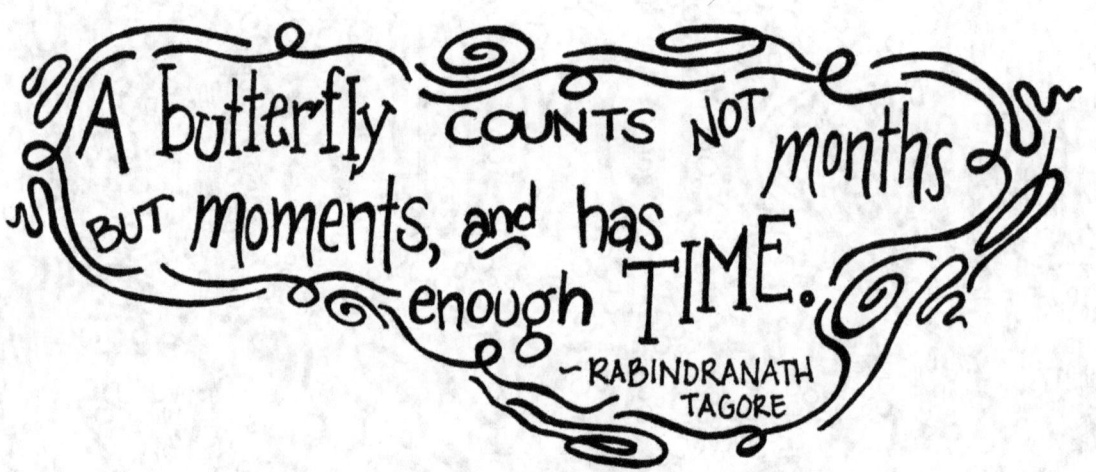

A butterfly counts not months but moments, and has enough TIME.

— RABINDRANATH TAGORE

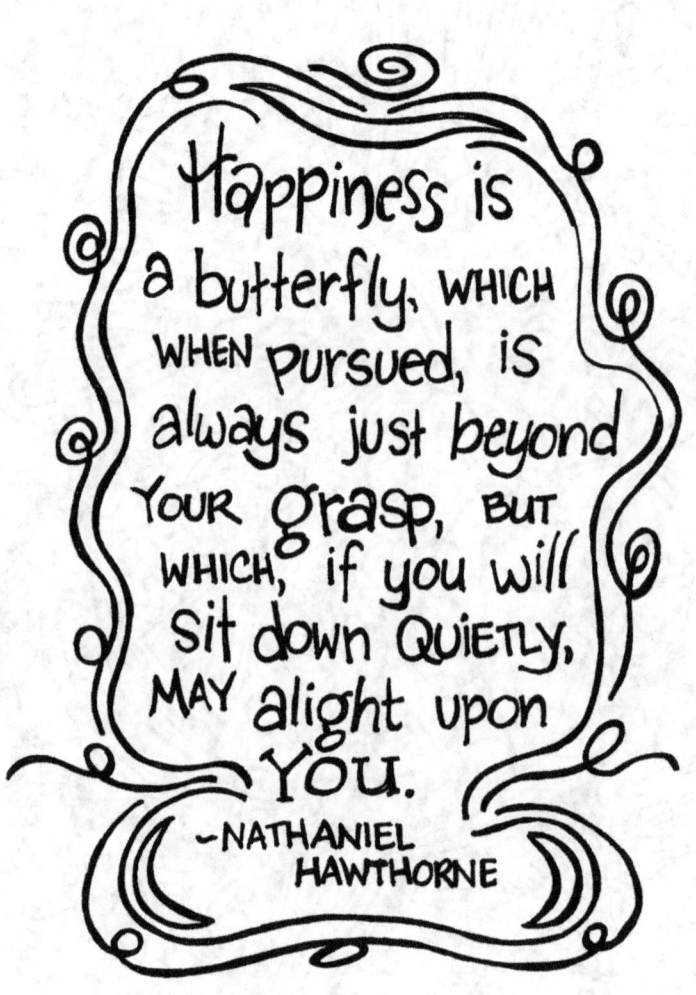

Happiness is a butterfly, WHICH WHEN pursued, is always just beyond YOUR grasp, BUT WHICH, if you will sit down QUIETLY, MAY alight upon YOU.

-NATHANIEL HAWTHORNE

A butterfly's wings move in a figure eight motion.

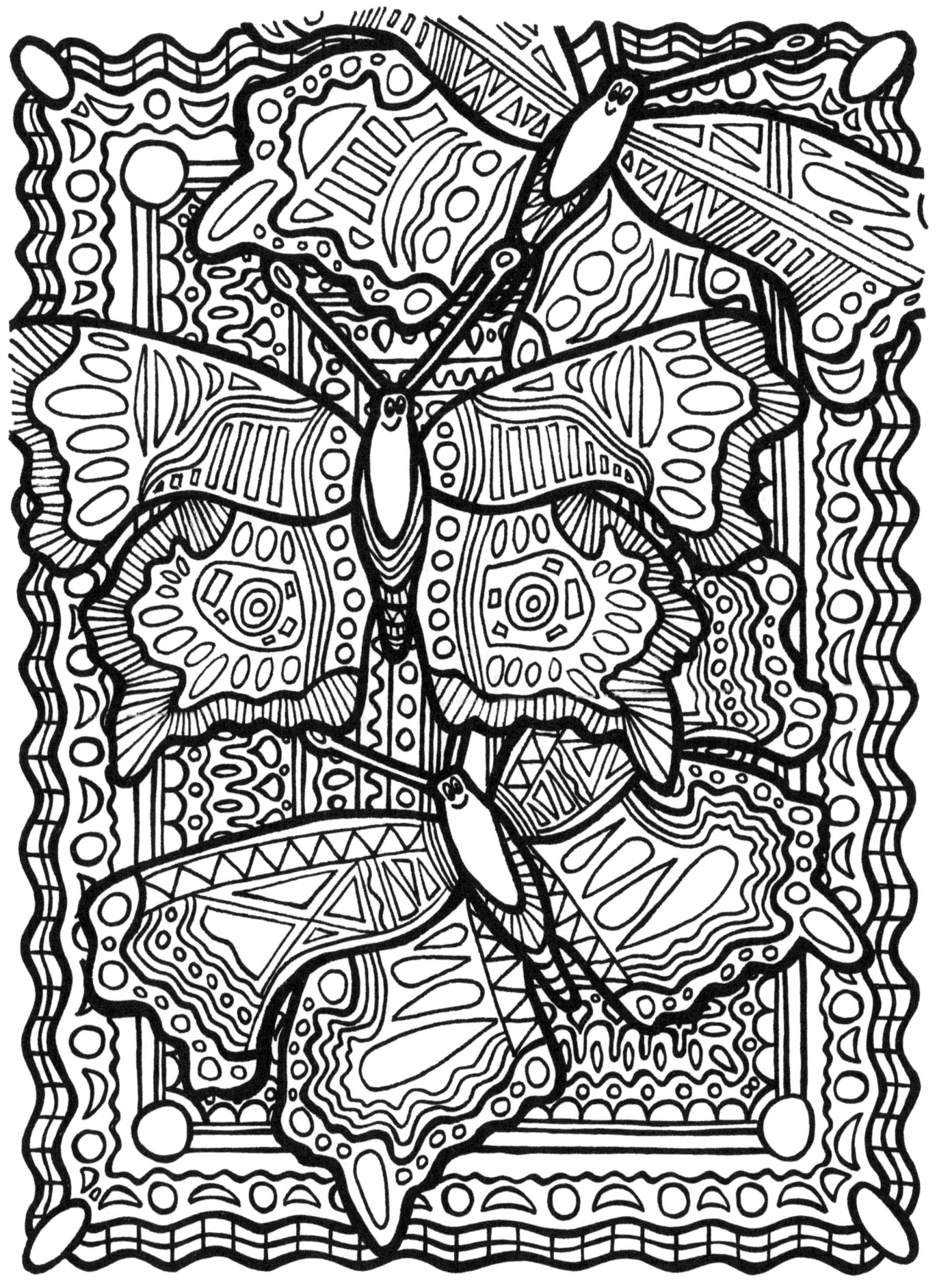

group of butterflies is called a flutter.

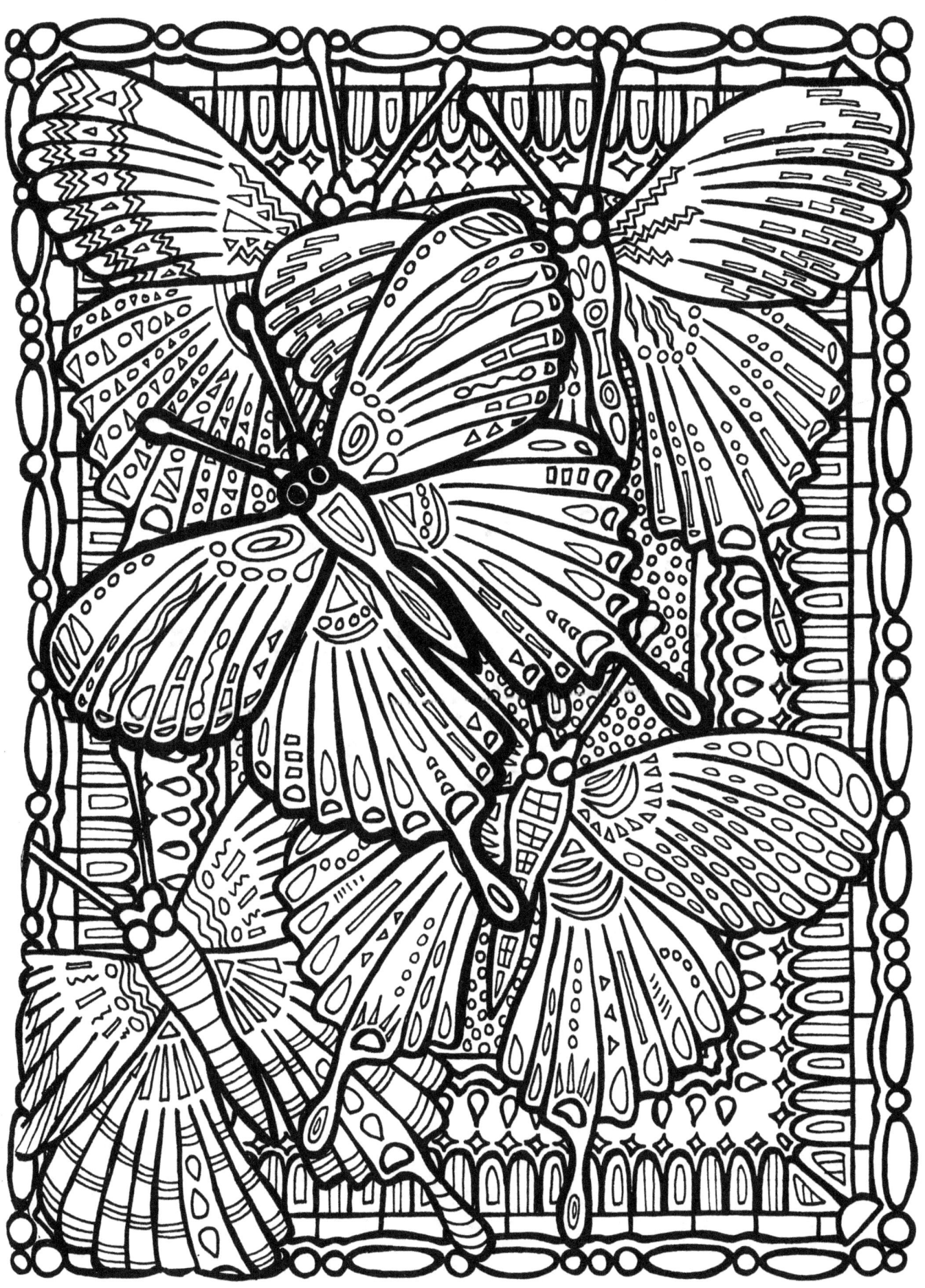

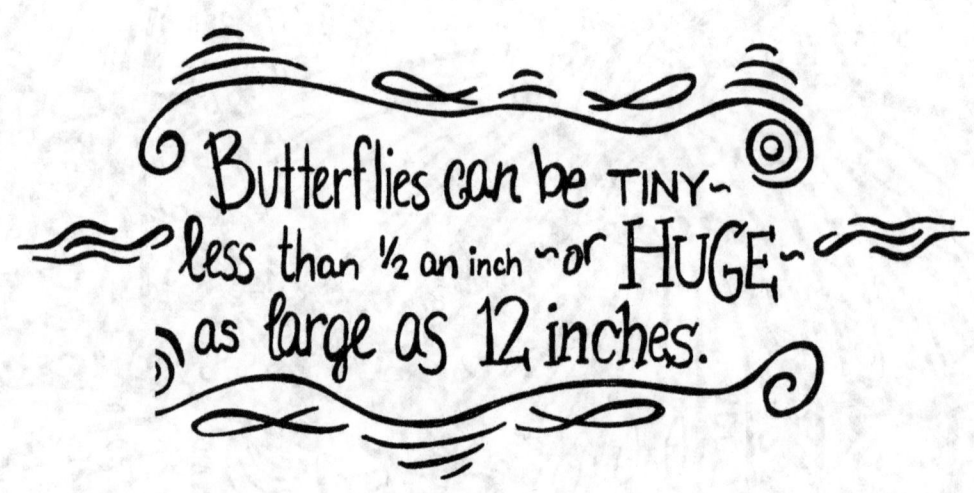

Butterflies can be TINY~
less than ½ an inch ~or HUGE~
as large as 12 inches.

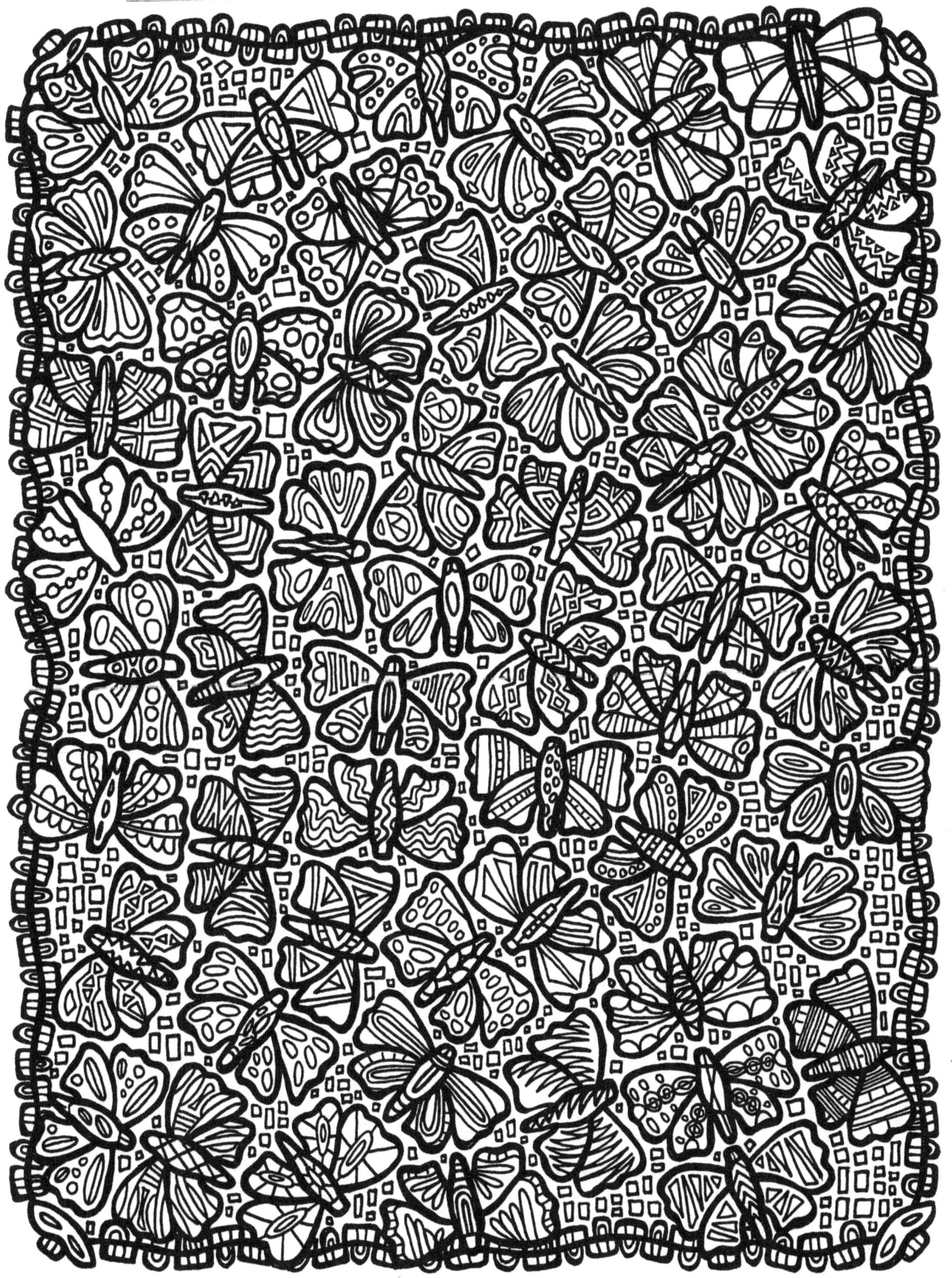

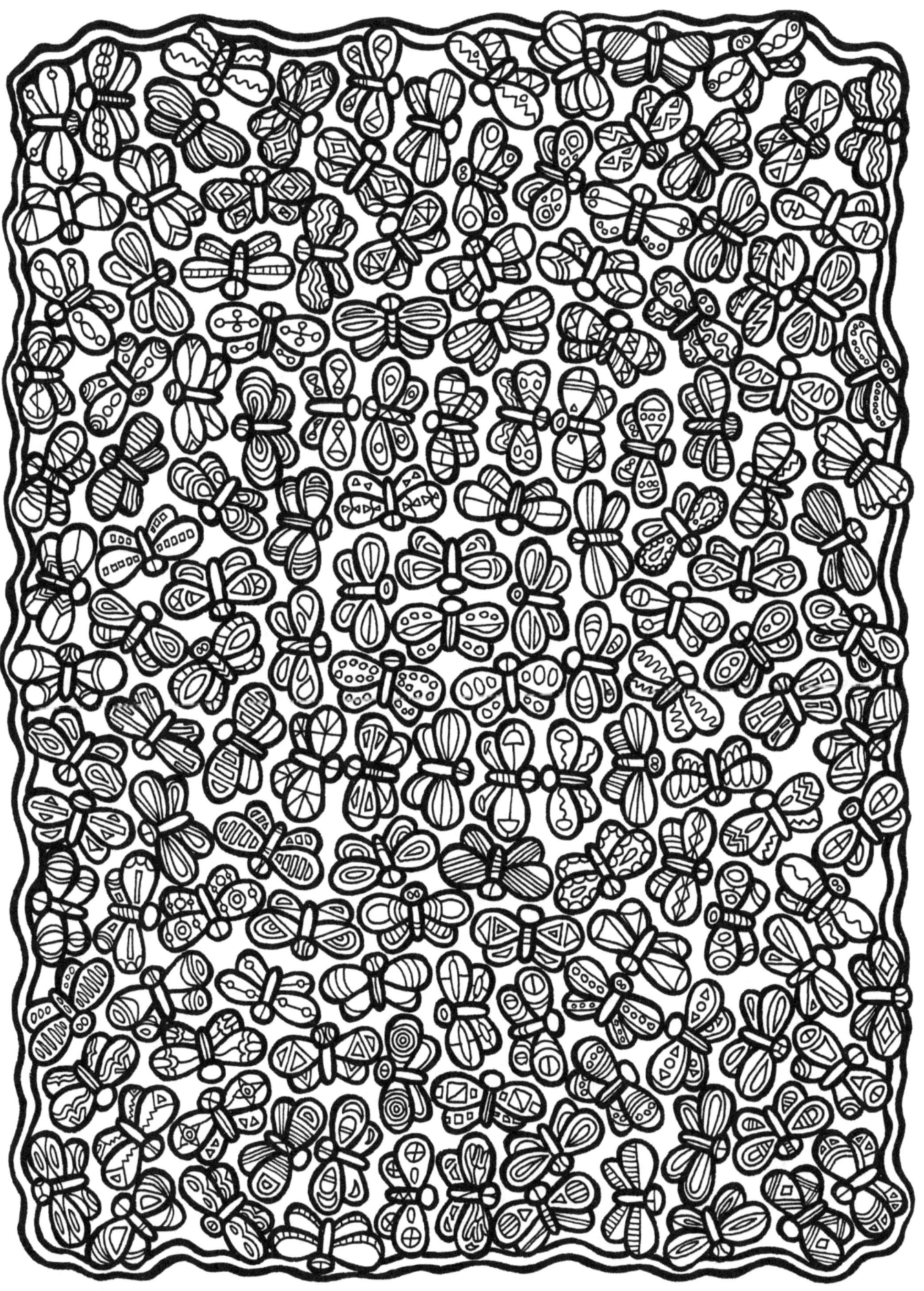

Ladybird beetles bring good fortune

Many SCARAB BEETLES are brightly colored, iridescent OR HAVE A metallic sheen.

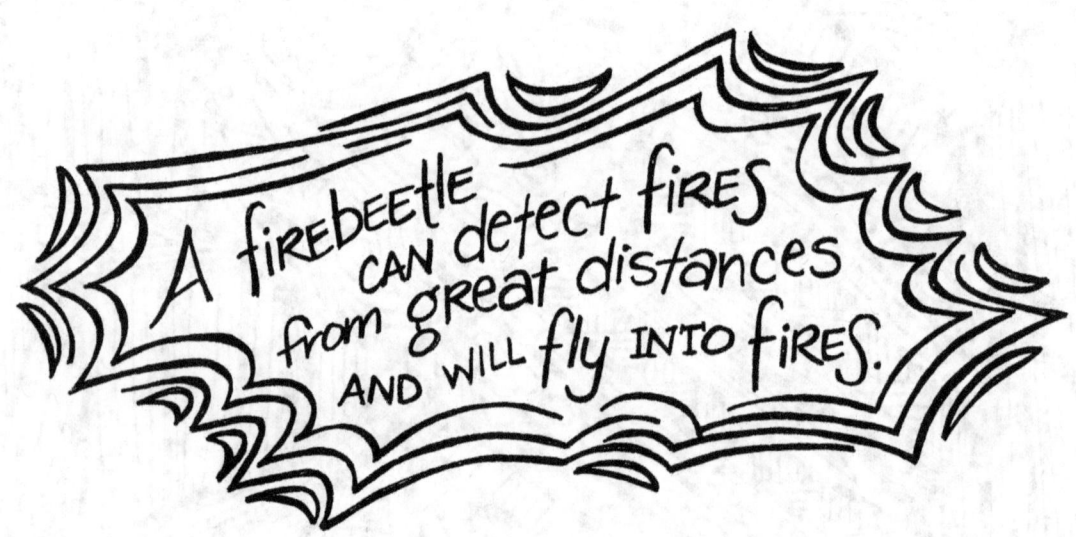

A firebeetle can detect fires from great distances and will fly into fires.

The STAG beetle is the LARGEST insect in the U.K. - IT CAN BECOME more than 10 cm in LENGTH.

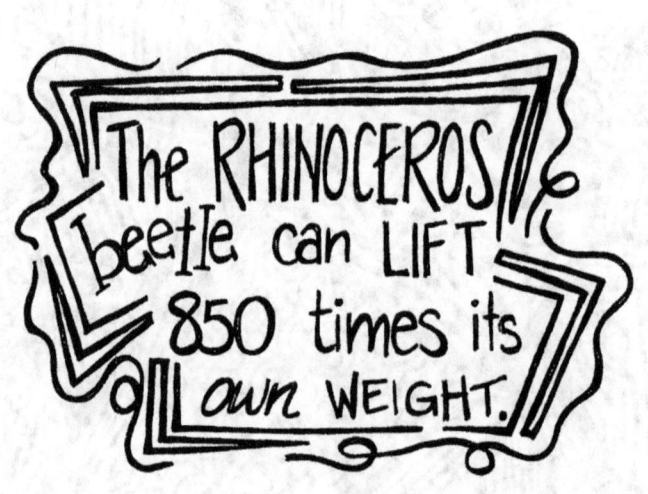

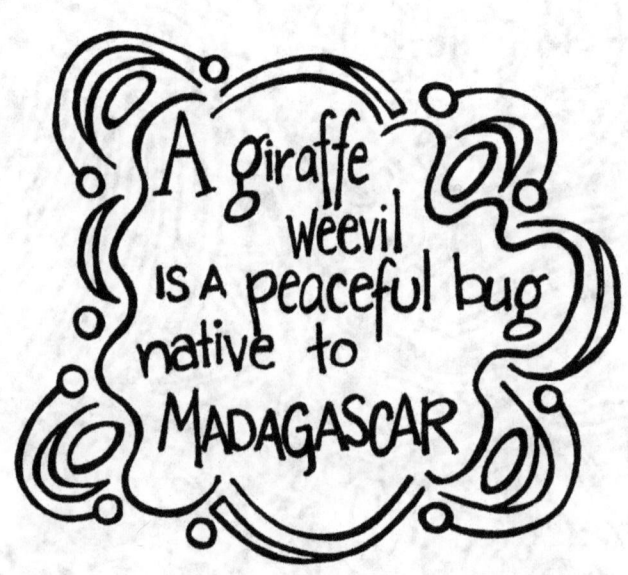

A giraffe weevil is a peaceful bug native to MADAGASCAR

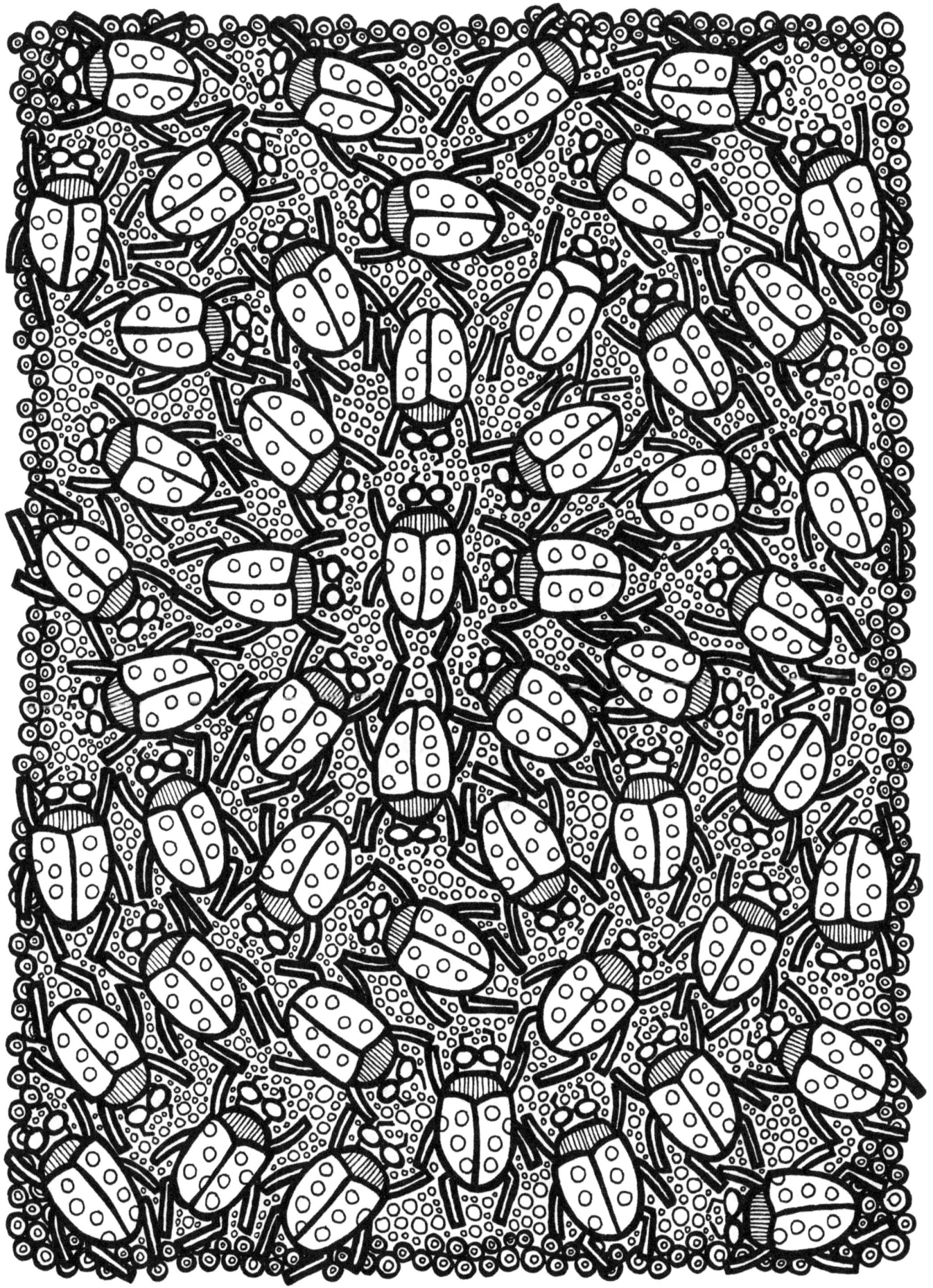

Scarab beetles roll balls of dung with their hind legs.

Honeybees visit 50-100 flowers during a collection trip.

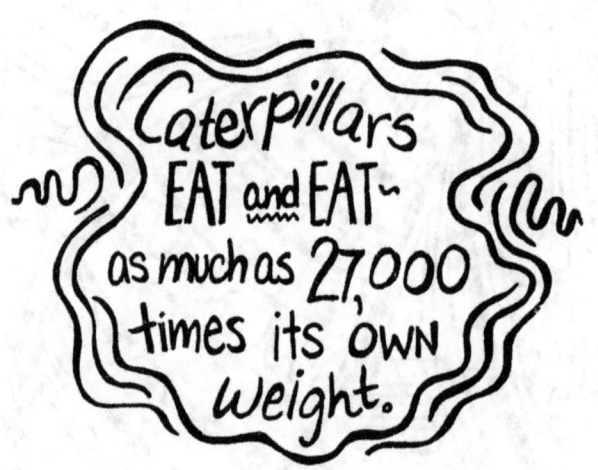

Caterpillars EAT and EAT~ as much as 27,000 times its own weight.

300 million years ago, dragonflies were more than 2 feet BIG.

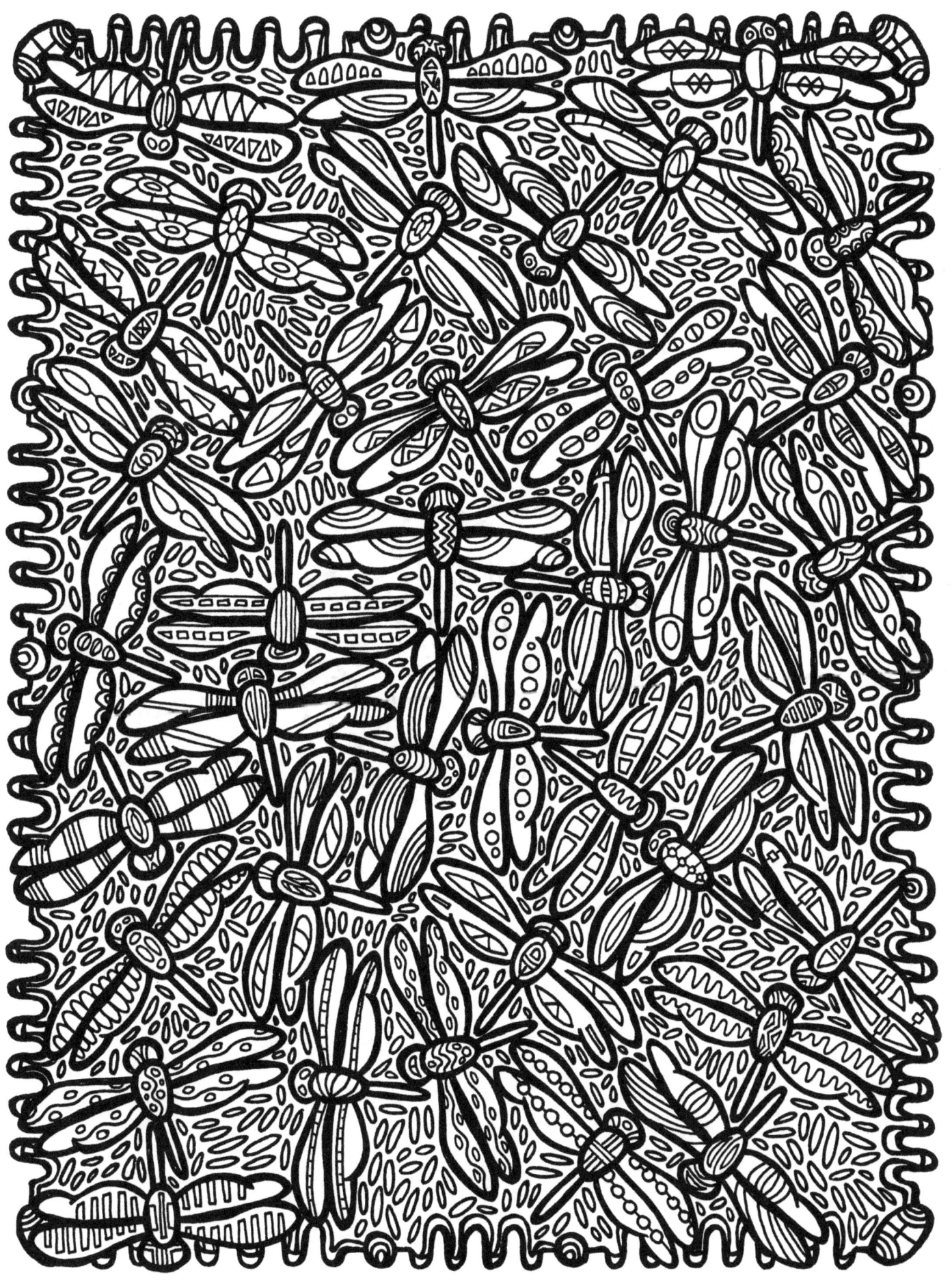

Dragonflies AMBUSH their PREY in the AIR

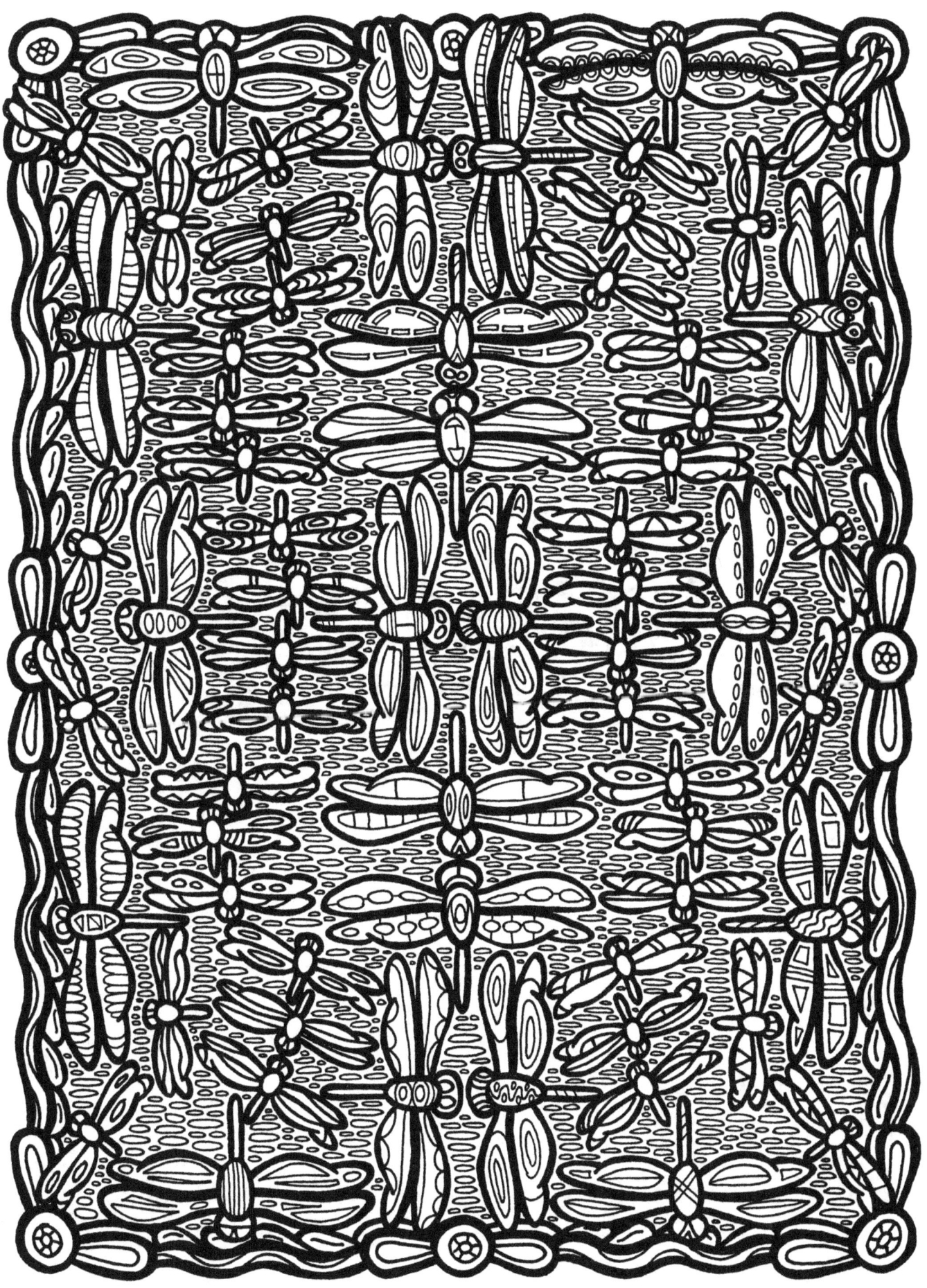

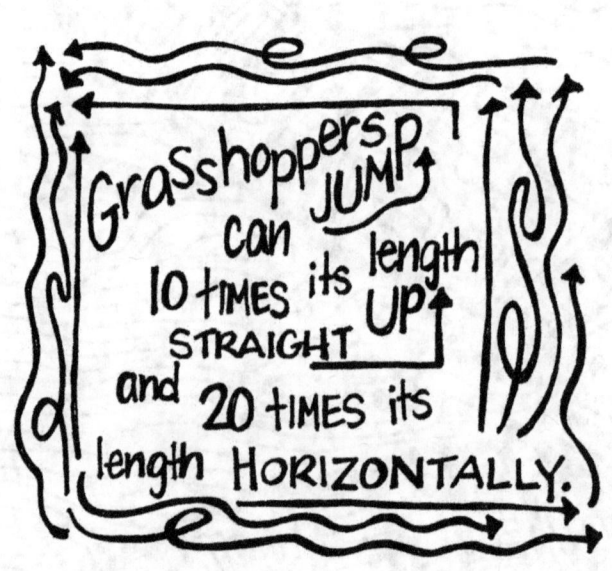

A hoverfly HOVERS above flowers and is a great pollinator.

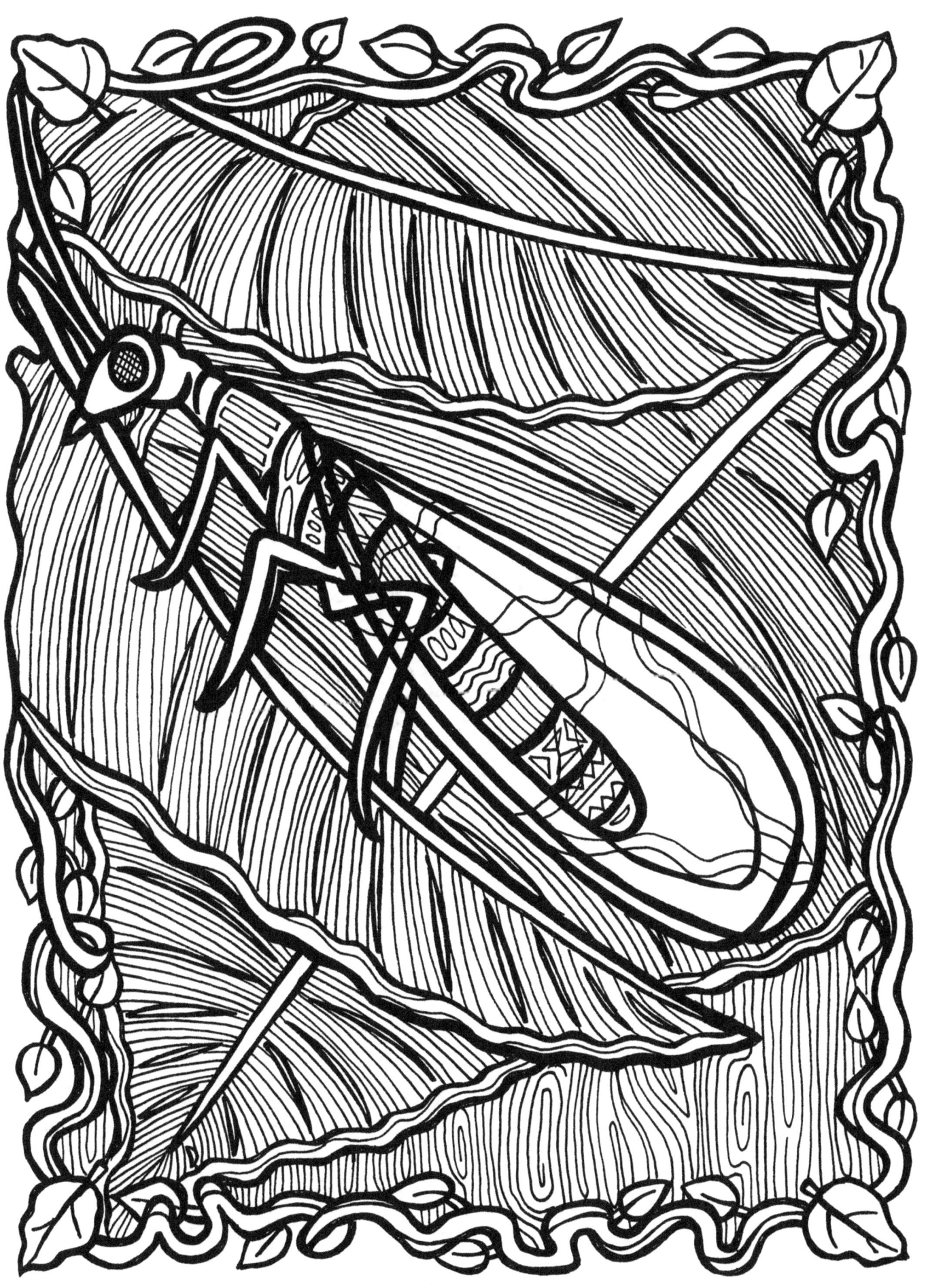

A praying mantis can swivel its head 180 degrees.

SNAILS are one of the SLOWEST creatures~ only moving about ½ inch per SECOND.

A STICK BUG can AVOID an ATTACK by giving up a LEG.

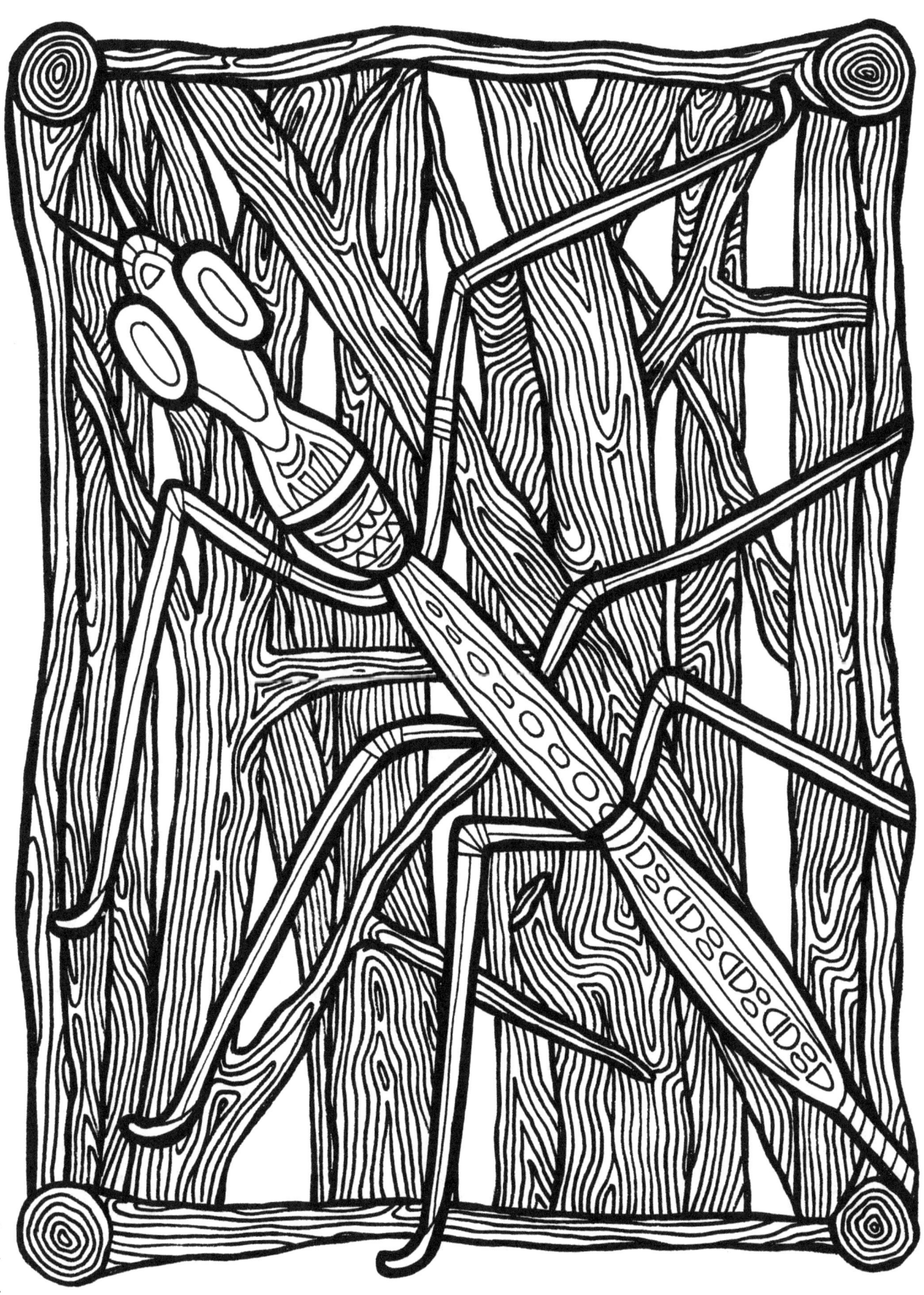

www.ingramcontent.com/pod-product-compliance
Lightning Source LLC
Chambersburg PA
CBHW081240280526
45787CB00006B/2733